What Is Rain?

Alan Trussell-Cullen

Dominie Press, Inc.

Publisher: Christine Yuen
Series Editors: Adria F. Klein & Alan Trussell-Cullen
Editor: Bob Rowland
Designers: Gary Hamada & Lois Stanfield

Photo Credits: SuperStock (Pages 4, 6, 8, 14, 16–Plant in Rain);
Simon Young (Pages 10, 16–Child Washing Hands, 17, 18).

Copyright ©2001 Dominie Press, Inc. All rights reserved. No part of this publication may be reproduced or transmitted in any form or by any means without permission in writing from the publisher. Reproduction of any part of this book, through photocopy, recording, or any electronic or mechanical retrieval system, without the written permission of the publisher, is an infringement of the copyright law.

Published by:

ꝑ Dominie Press, Inc.

1949 Kellogg Avenue
Carlsbad, California 92008 USA

www.dominie.com

ISBN 0-7685-0576-3

Printed in Singapore

17 V0ZF 14 13

Table of Contents

What Is Rain?	4
Light Rain	6
Heavy Rain	7
Hail	8
Lots of Rain Here	12
Not Much Rain Here	14
Who Needs Rain?	16
Our Word Wall about Rain	18
Picture Glossary	19
Index	20

Rain is water that falls
in drops from the sky.

Sometimes the rain is light. We call this a shower.

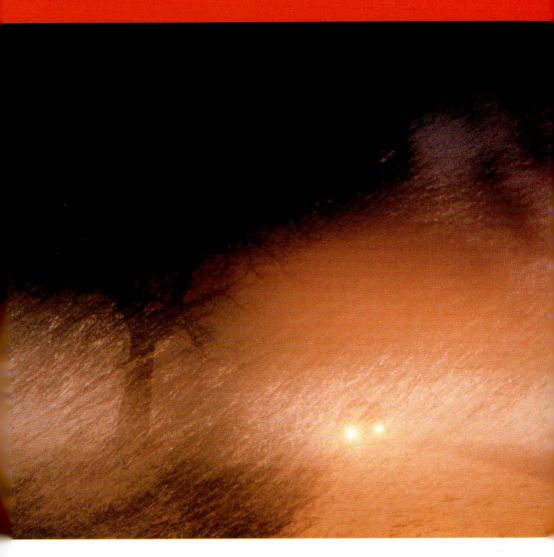

Sometimes the rain is heavy.
We call this a rainstorm.

Sometimes raindrops freeze and become pieces of ice.

We call this hail.

We measured the rain
that fell on our playground
this week.

Lots of rain falls
in some parts of the world.

It usually rains every day
in a tropical rainforest.

In other parts of the world,
very little rain falls.

Rain hardly ever falls
in a desert.

Plants need rain to grow.

People need rain, too. We need rain to give us water for washing.

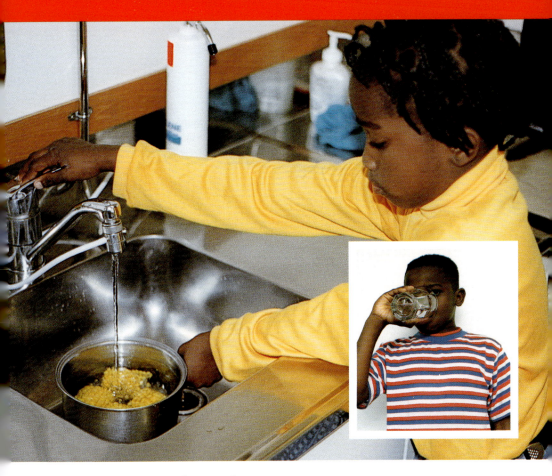

We need rain
to give us water for cooking.
We need rain
to give us water for drinking.

Our Word Wall about Rain.

drips	umbrella	puddle	drops
showers	splash	pool	
wet	rainbow	downpour	flood
weather	hailstones	drizzle	
trickle	raincoat	drinking water	soaked
drenched	monsoon	storm	

We collected words that have something to do with rain.

We made a word wall about rain.

Picture Glossary

desert:

ice: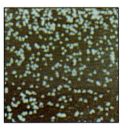

hail:

rain:

Index

desert, 15

hail, 9

ice, 8

plants, 16

rain, 5, 6, 7, 11, 13, 15, 16, 17, 18

rainstorm, 7

shower, 6

word wall, 18